Contents

JOSEPH

HOW GOD BUILDS CHARACTER

PAUL
BORTHWICK

9 STUDIES
FOR INDIVIDUALS
OR GROUPS

Life
Builder
Study

INTER-VARSITY PRESS
36 Causton Street, London SW1P 4ST, England
Email: ivp@ivpbooks.com
Website: www.ivpbooks.com

Originally published in the United States of America in the LifeGuide® Bible Studies series in 2003 by InterVarsity Press, Downers Grove, Illinois
First published in Great Britain by Scripture Union in 2004
This edition published in Great Britain by Inter-Varsity Press 2019

British Library Cataloguing-in-Publication Data
A catalogue record for this book is available from the British Library.

ISBN: 978–1–78359–859–5

Printed in Great Britain by Ashford Colour Press Ltd, Gosport, Hampshire

Inter-Varsity Press publishes Christian books that are true to the Bible and that communicate the gospel, develop discipleship and strengthen the church for its mission in the world.

IVP originated within the Inter-Varsity Fellowship, now the Universities and Colleges Christian Fellowship, a student movement connecting Christian Unions in universities and colleges throughout Great Britain, and a member movement of the International Fellowship of Evangelical Students. Website: www.uccf.org.uk. That historic association is maintained, and all senior IVP staff and committee members subscribe to the UCCF Basis of Faith.

Getting the Most Out of *Joseph*

Several years ago, I came across Chuck Swindoll's book *Joseph: A Man of Integrity and Forgiveness* (Nashville: Word, 1998). Joseph was already one of my favorite biblical characters, so it did not take much convincing to get me to buy the book. The subtitle really confirmed my decision. I thought to myself, *That's the kind of person I want to be!*

Both words speak to the issue of spiritual depth. A person of character—especially in the context of the Christian life—sets himself or herself apart from others by moral uprightness, ethical courage and the strength to stand against evil. Integrity takes character a step further. Warren Wiersbe writes:

> Integrity is to personal or corporate character what health is to the body or 20/20 vision is to the eyes. A person with integrity is not divided (that's duplicity) or merely pretending (that's hypocrisy). He or she is "whole"; life is "put together," and things are working together harmoniously. People with integrity have nothing to hide and nothing to fear. Their lives are open books. They are integers. (*The Integrity Crisis* [Nashville: Oliver-Nelson, 1988], p. 21)

People who have integrity live integrated lives. Their life convictions and their lifestyles match. What they say they believe gets worked out in the way that they live. Their actions, values and behavior stay consistent—whether celebrating Sunday worship with the fellowship of the faithful or transacting business on Monday in the marketplace. Their character distinguishes itself by consistency— whether relating to family and friends on weeknights, or retreating to moments of isolation where only God sees their actions.

Dr. Martyn Lloyd-Jones tells the tragic story of the young preacher who preached so well yet lived such an immoral life that people "wished that when he was in the pulpit he wouldn't leave, and when he was out of the pulpit, he'd never return." The problem? He lacked integrity. His teaching and his behavior were not integrated.

Isn't integrity what every follower of Jesus Christ desires? To be known as a person of deep and honest character? To be characterized as a person of consistent behavior that reflects Christ in us—no matter what the circumstances?

That's why this study guide takes us into an in-depth examination of the family, experiences, choices and impact of the life of Old Testament Joseph, one of the twelve sons of Israel. He is known as a dreamer, the possessor of the "coat of many colors" and the key character of the musical *Joseph and the Amazing Technicolor Dreamcoat.*

But there is much more to Joseph—so much more that Joseph's story in the book of Genesis takes up more chapters than Adam, Noah, Abraham, Isaac or Jacob. Genesis 37 and then 39—50 focus primarily on the life of Joseph. In the studies that follow, we'll explore these chapters in an effort to discover what Joseph's life teaches us, several millennia later, about being people of character and integrity.

Suggestions for Individual Study

1. As you begin each study, pray that God will speak to you through his Word.

2. Read the introduction to the study and respond to the personal reflection question or exercise. This is designed to help you focus on God and on the theme of the study.

3. Each study deals with a particular passage—so that you can delve into the author's meaning in that context. Read and reread the passage to be studied. The questions are written using the language of the New International Version, so you may wish to use that version of the Bible. The New Revised Standard Version is also recommended.

4. This is an inductive Bible study, designed to help you discover for yourself what Scripture is saying. The study includes three types of questions. *Observation* questions ask about the basic facts: who, what, when, where and how. *Interpretation* questions delve into the meaning of the passage. *Application* questions help you discover the implications of the text for growing in Christ. These three keys unlock the treasures of Scripture.

Write your answers to the questions in the spaces provided or in a personal journal. Writing can bring clarity and deeper understanding of yourself and of God's Word.

5. It might be good to have a Bible dictionary handy. Use it to look up any unfamiliar words, names or places.

6. Use the prayer suggestion to guide you in thanking God for what you have learned and to pray about the applications that have come to mind.

7. You may want to go on to the suggestion under "Now or Later," or you may want to use that idea for your next study.

Suggestions for Members of a Group Study

1. Come to the study prepared. Follow the suggestions for individual study mentioned above. You will find that careful preparation will greatly enrich your time spent in group discussion.

2. Be willing to participate in the discussion. The leader of your group will not be lecturing. Instead, he or she will be encouraging the members of the group to discuss what they have learned. The leader will be asking the questions that are found in this guide.

3. Stick to the topic being discussed. Your answers should be based on the verses which are the focus of the discussion and not on outside authorities such as commentaries or speakers. These studies focus on a particular passage of Scripture. Only rarely should you refer to other portions of the Bible. This allows for everyone to participate in in-depth study on equal ground.

4. Be sensitive to the other members of the group. Listen attentively when they describe what they have learned. You may be surprised by their insights! Each question assumes a variety of answers. Many questions do not have "right" answers, particularly questions that aim at meaning or application. Instead the questions push us to explore the passage more thoroughly.

When possible, link what you say to the comments of others. Also, be affirming whenever you can. This will encourage some of the more hesitant members of the group to participate.

5. Be careful not to dominate the discussion. We are sometimes so eager to express our thoughts that we leave too little opportunity for others to respond. By all means participate! But allow others to also.

6. Expect God to teach you through the passage being discussed and through the other members of the group. Pray that you will have an enjoyable and profitable time together, but also that as a result of the study you will find ways that you can take action individually and/or as a group.

7. Remember that anything said in the group is considered confidential and should not be discussed outside the group unless specific permission is given to do so.

8. If you are the group leader, you will find additional suggestions at the back of the guide.

1

Building on Damaged Foundations

> ## *Genesis 29:14—30:24; 37:1-4*

Did you ever wish that you had come from a different family? Are there things about your family background and your growing-up years that you'd change if you could? If your answer is yes, you are not alone. Many of us—even if we love our families deeply—speculate how life would be different if certain situations from our childhood were changed.

GROUP DISCUSSION. Think about your growth years at home—before the age of eighteen. As you reflect on the impact of your childhood and family background on the person you are now, what trait or characteristic that you learned are you most grateful for? What trait or characteristic would you most like to change?

PERSONAL REFLECTION. If you were to ask God one question about the childhood that you've lived, what would you ask him?

Often we think that being a person of depth, character or integrity comes easiest to those who grew up in perfect family situations with wonderful parents in nurturing homes. Our introduction to Joseph and his family sets the stage for quite a different scenario. *Read Genesis 29:14—30:24.*

1. Outline Joseph's family structure as revealed in these verses—dad, moms, sons.

2. What do these verses reveal about Joseph's family life?

3. Imagine growing up in Joseph's family. What interpersonal dynamics can you most identify with from your own family?

4. What conditions set the tone for Joseph being Jacob's favorite son?

5. *Read Genesis 37:1-4.* Joseph served as a shepherd with his half-brothers (same father, different mothers). Imagine this blended family living and working in virtual isolation in a desert community. What relational or interpersonal dynamics might you expect to find in a normal day of work?

6. Imagine yourself as one of the other brothers of Joseph. Given what you know from these verses, how would you have felt toward Joseph?

toward your father?

Have you ever had similar struggles with your own family members?

7. What might have motivated Joseph to bring a bad report to his father about his brothers?

8. What did Jacob (Israel), Joseph's father, do that also could have intensified the rivalry?

What do you think this action meant to Joseph?

What do you think it meant to his brothers?

9. How did the brothers demonstrate that all was not well between themselves and brother Joseph?

10. As you look at your own family background and relational experiences, what negative factors can you identify that make you wonder if God can ever use your life now?

11. Reflect on your life. What circumstances in your past (that were out of your control) serve to make you feel bitter or angry toward your parents?

toward God?

12. Romans 15:4 states that "whatever was written in earlier times was written for our instruction, that through perseverance and the encouragement of the Scriptures we might have hope." How does the background story of Joseph and his family encourage you?

Ask God to begin the work of healing you from whatever wounds may exist from your past, and ask God to help you release bitterness toward others that hampers your relationships now.

Now or Later

Take some time to write about or reflect on areas in your family upbringing that still bring you pain today. Pray through each area and then ask yourself:

Which of these areas require me simply to let go and forgive someone from my heart?

Which of these areas do I need to take action on by doing something that can bridge the gap between me and a sibling or me and a parent?

What action will I take toward healing these relationships?

2

Dreams, Visions and Discretion

Genesis 37:5-11

Does an encounter with God or a vital relationship with God guarantee that our personal problems will be solved? We'd all like to think so, but experience teaches us something quite different. Often the deeper one grows spiritually, the more intense the problems of life become.

GROUP DISCUSSION. Why do you think that one often experiences greater hardships in his or her life when in a deeper relationship with Christ?

PERSONAL REFLECTION. Think through your own family relationships and primary friendships. How has being a follower of Jesus affected these relationships? What are the benefits and the stresses?

While we don't know many specifics about Joseph's relationship with God, we do know that God intervened in his life at age seventeen and changed his life, his relationships and his future in an incredible way. *Read Genesis 37:5-11.*

1. Look carefully at the content of Joseph's two dreams. What emotions would you feel as you woke up remembering these dreams?

---

2. How would you have reacted if you were one of the brothers hearing this dream?

---

3. With such a bad environment at home (remember Genesis 37:1-4), why would Joseph have reported these dreams—especially given that their interpretation was fairly obvious?

---

4. If you were Joseph (and did not know what the outcome would be), would you have shared your dream with your brothers or father? Why or why not?

---

5. Describe Jacob's reaction to the dream. Why do you think he reacted differently than the brothers?

---

6. What does this passage teach us about the character of Joseph at this point?

---

7. What is the role of supernatural dreams in the life of the Christian?

8. What's the difference between having a dream and having a "vision" for our life?

---

9. How do we determine the difference between a dream that is caused by our psyche or our settings and a dream that comes from God?

---

10. Reach back in your memory to age seventeen. What were you dreaming then?

What dreams seem now to be simply products of youthfulness?

---

11. What past or present dreams would you like to see God fulfill?

Invite God to intervene in your life. Ask him to give you a life dream or vision that is bigger than anything you can accomplish on your own.

Now or Later

What are your dreams or visions for your life? Take a few hours apart with your Bible and a notebook in the week ahead. Sit quietly before God. Ask him to give you new dreams or visions about your life.

3

Leaving Your Dream with God

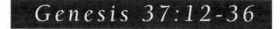

Genesis 37:12-36

People with dreams, visions or great ideas often end up unfulfilled because they lack the strength of character to wait to see their dreams realized. Even when God gives us ideas or dreams or visions, it may take time to see the fulfillment. God first wants to develop our patience and dependence on him.

GROUP DISCUSSION. Describe a time in your own life when you wanted an answer and God instead taught you patience.

PERSONAL REFLECTION. Think through the unanswered prayers of your own life or the unanswered questions that you're bringing before God. Why do you think God makes you wait? What is he teaching you about yourself? What is he teaching you about your relationship with him?

Joseph's father had set him apart as the family leader. Joseph had dreams of being a great leader. But he never could have predicted the next steps that God would take him through. *Read Genesis 37:12-28.*

1. What do verses 12-17 tell you about how roles have changed now in the family of Israel (compare against Genesis 37:2)?

2. What thoughts and feelings about Joseph might have gone through the minds of the brothers as he arrived at the place where they were working?

3. What is the effect of bitterness on our perspective on others and our ability to relate to others?

4. What evidence is there that God is intervening on Joseph's behalf?

5. What do you think motivated Reuben's efforts to rescue Joseph?

6. Put yourself in Joseph's sandals. As the brothers were talking and your life and future were being discussed, what emotions would you have been going through?

How might you have related to God?

---

7. *Read Genesis 37:29-36.* Return again to the issue of bitterness. What is the effect of the brothers' vengeful action against Joseph on their relationship with Reuben?

with their father?

with God?

---

8. Why is the loss so severe for Jacob?

9. Imagine the emotions of Joseph as he goes from his father's favorite son with big dreams to being sold as a slave to ending up on the slave crew of Potiphar in Egypt. What would you have been praying to God during these days?

---

10. From the perspective of the brothers, how does this passage challenge you regarding bitterness or unresolved conflicts in your own relationships?

---

11. From Joseph's perspective, what does this passage teach you about leaving your dreams in God's hands?

---

12. What do you do when you think that God is guiding you one way and you come to a twist in the road that totally confuses you?

Ask God to give you patience and perseverance to go through whatever tough times he may have ahead of you as you seek to fulfill his purposes in your own life.

Now or Later

Memorize Psalm 27:13-14 to encourage your patience in waiting on God.

4

Sexual Purity

When All Else Fails—Run!

Genesis 39:6-20

Character is often described as being "tested." To describe someone as having "tested character" means that he or she has demonstrated moral fortitude in the face of temptation or has served nobly in the face of severe hardship.

GROUP DISCUSSION. What contemporary or historical person do you respect as a person of character and why?

PERSONAL REFLECTION. In the attitude of prayer and quietness, ask yourself this question: when am I most vulnerable to temptation? in times of loneliness? in times following great success? other times?

We now find Joseph serving as a slave in the household of the powerful Egyptian Potiphar, captain of Pharaoh's guard and—according to historians—the chief executioner in Pharaoh's courts. Joseph has ascended in the slave ranks (something we'll examine in the next study), but in this part of Joseph's story, we find him in the face of temptation. *Read Genesis 39:6-20.*

1. How do you respond to this vivid and detailed story of Joseph's temptation?

2. Why would Potiphar's wife, a woman of high culture and refinement, be attracted to a slave like Joseph?

3. Imagine yourself in Joseph's position. Why might you be tempted to think that saying yes to this woman could be a good thing?

4. What types of temptation are most likely to sway you?

5. Look closely at verses 7-12. In what various ways did Joseph resist?

6. What were Joseph's reasons for resistance?

What do his reasons teach you about resisting temptation—even when no one's looking?

7. In the face of the most severe seduction from Potiphar's wife, how does Joseph resist?

8. What details does the writer give us that hint at the fact that Joseph might have been close to succumbing to her advances?

---

9. Joseph does the right thing, maintains his moral high ground and resists temptation. Yet notice where his uprightness gets him! If you were Joseph, what questions would you have for God at this point?

---

10. After hearing his wife's accusation, Potiphar, chief of the executioners, throws Joseph into the king's (white-collar) prison. Why didn't he just have the defenseless Hebrew slave killed?

---

11. What does Joseph's story teach you about facing temptation?

---

12. What does Joseph's story teach you about the potential results of obeying God?

Ask God for the strength of the Holy Spirit to enable you to resist temptation of any form when it comes—especially when you're alone.

Now or Later

Contrast the story of Joseph with the account of the young man in Proverbs 7:6-27—another young man who faced a temptress. Identify the points of decision in each story that led one to resist sexual temptation and the other to succumb.

5

The Integrity
of a Servant

Genesis 39:1-6, 20-23

Resisting temptation for a moment might be simply a matter of running from it, but what do we do with out-of-control circumstances that linger for months or years? How do we maintain character when we start wondering, "God, what are your purposes in this mess that I'm in?"

GROUP DISCUSSION. As followers of Jesus Christ, what is our responsibility for our attitudes and our motivations, especially if we find ourselves in oppressive conditions?

PERSONAL REFLECTION. What would be the most difficult freedom for you to lose? If you lost it, how do you think that loss would affect your relationship with God?

Joseph has undergone some traumatic changes. At age seventeen, he's reveling in dreams, sitting in the place of honor in the household and enjoying being the apple of his father's eye. Suddenly, in just days, he finds himself as a slave in a foreign land. *Read Genesis 39:1-6.*

---

1. Imagine yourself in Joseph's new world. List all of the changes that you now face.

2. What sets Joseph apart in the eyes of his master?

3. In the last study, we saw that Joseph did what was right and resisted Potiphar's wife, and it landed him in prison. In this account, Joseph also does what is right; what are the results this time?

4. The writer describes Joseph the slave as a "successful" man (39:2). What do you think this suggests about God's definition of success?

5. *Read Genesis 39:20-23.* We now find Joseph in prison, unjustly accused. What are the parallels between his experience as a slave in Potiphar's house and now as a prisoner in the king's prison?

6. Imagine you are the chief prison guard. What kinds of things might have made Joseph stand apart from other prisoners?

7. In verses 22-23 we see that Joseph is now responsible for the care of the other prisoners. Genesis 40:4 tells us that he "attended" the other prisoners as a servant might. In what ways might it have been challenging for Joseph to care for others as a prisoner himself?

8. In both the house of Pharaoh and in the prison, we read that "the LORD was with Joseph." What does this phrase signify—both in describing the relationship of Joseph to God and the relationship of Joseph to his work (Genesis 39:2-6, 21, 23)?

9. Given all of the circumstances of your life—community, workplace, school, household—what would make other people look at your life and say, "Wow, the Lord is with him or her?"

10. "The pit" plays a big part in Joseph's life (Genesis 37:19, 22, 24 and Genesis 40:15 [dungeon]). What role does the "pit" play in character development?

What pits has God brought you out of?

When you find you're still in a "pit" (and God hasn't brought you out), how does it challenge your willingness to serve?

Ask God for grace to be a servant to others—even if you're in circumstances that you would never have chosen for yourself.

Now or Later

The book of Philippians describes the life and perspective of another unjustly imprisoned man of God, Paul the apostle. Read through this book and look for parallels between Paul's attitudes and Joseph's.

6

Discernment

Serving others often involves helping them understand what God is saying to them through their experiences. But it also involves listening, seeking God on behalf of others and sometimes confronting people with tough truth.

GROUP DISCUSSION. What experiences have you had with either confronting someone or being confronted by someone regarding tough truth?

PERSONAL REFLECTION. Journal or pray about situations or experiences in your life that are mysteries to you—in which you really do not know what God is saying. Then ask God for a discerning spirit to enable you to understand his purposes.

In this study, we join Joseph as he rises to a new challenge as interpreter of dreams and reporter of harsh messages. Joseph continues in his role as "chief prisoner," but in this study, he gets launched into a new role that will eventually put him in the high courts of Egypt with the Pharaoh. *Read Genesis 40:1-8.*

---

1. Describe the mindset and emotions of the four men cited in these verses.

2. Who do you most identify with and why?

---

3. What surprises you about Joseph's response in verse 8?

---

4. *Read Genesis 40:9-23.* How would it have felt to hear Joseph's interpretation if you were the cupbearer?

if you were the baker?

---

5. We get a glimpse of Joseph's personal feelings in verses 14-15. What does his request tell you?

---

6. Verse 23 tells us the cupbearer "forgot him." If you were in Joseph's position, what emotions would have surfaced?

---

7. *Read Genesis 41:1-32.* What highlights of this part of the story would you emphasize if you were summarizing it to someone in three minutes?

---

8. Notice 41:16. Why was it important for Joseph to make this point?

9. Assuming that the spirit of discernment requires a clear mind and spirit, how do you think Joseph overcame his feelings toward the cupbearer as they stood there together before the Pharaoh?

10. If you were the prisoner Joseph standing before the person you perceived to be the most powerful person on earth, how would you have felt about making the statements in verses 26-27?

11. Why are we sometimes hesitant to offer the bold discernment of Joseph when we're interpreting things like dreams, world events or even personal experiences?

12. To develop wise discernment like Joseph, what changes do you need to make in your life or what characteristics do you need to develop?

Pray for the spirit of discernment so that you might better serve others.

Now or Later

Do an in-depth study on the topic of discernment, starting with Hebrews 5:14. Investigate what the writer in Hebrews means by "solid food" as well as "constant use," and then explore ways that you can train your senses to discern good versus evil.

7

Long-Range Planning

People who make an impact on others are usually long-term people; that is, the effect of their life, their character or their integrity is neither momentary nor instant, but over a long period.

GROUP DISCUSSION. Think of some older Christian whose life and integrity you'd like to emulate. What are the long-term characteristics you see in that person?

PERSONAL REFLECTION. Are there areas of your life that have ever suffered because of poor long-term planning or the unwillingness to think long-term? Identify these and ask God to use Joseph's example to help you overcome procrastination and start planning.

Read Genesis 41:33-36 to get a picture of Joseph's approach to long-term investment.

1. How does Joseph let Pharaoh know that he is the man for the job?

2. Was Joseph being self-serving in making this suggestion? Why or why not?

3. *Read Genesis 41:37-45.* What do you think were the characteristics of Joseph that made him stand out so quickly before Pharaoh?

4. Put yourself in Joseph's situation: how would you have been feeling when you moved from the prison to the "second-in-command" chariot in one day?

5. What can you learn from Joseph's model about how to work for a pagan boss?

6. *Read Genesis 41:46-57.* How many years have transpired between Joseph's dream and subsequent enslavement in Egypt? What has kept Joseph going all this time?

7. Describe Joseph's long-range plan for Egypt.

8. When the tough times of famine come, what happens to Joseph's position of power in Egypt and even in the world?

9. How was Joseph feeling about his past hardships and present position?

10. How does a follower of Jesus Christ strike a balance between living in the moment—in response to the events that God brings into our lives—and planning ahead?

11. Joseph's long-term view of his life is obviously rewarded. How do you hope that God will reward you if you stay faithful to him over the long-term?

Ask God to give you plans for your life that only he can fulfill, and then ask him to help you start moving in that direction.

Now or Later

Using a concordance, do a word study in the book of Proverbs on the words *plan* and *planning*. Make a list of all the references in this book to the rewards, promises and perils related to diligent planning or failing to plan. Then, using these observations, make two or three applications on how your attitude toward or practice of long-range planning needs to change.

8

Forgiveness and Release

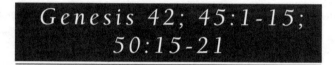

Genesis 42; 45:1-15; 50:15-21

Jesus came not only to restore the relationship between God and us but also to reconcile us to each other. The biblical concept of reconciliation carries with it the need for healed relationships.

GROUP DISCUSSION. If people in your past have hurt you deeply, should you forgive them even before they ask? Explain your thoughts.

How do you release the emotional hurt?

PERSONAL REFLECTION. Who in your life and past do you need to forgive? Ask God what steps you need to take toward inner healing and, if possible, healing the relationship.

Joseph is enjoying worldwide power and acclaim. He's "living large" in the palaces of Egypt, with prestige and wealth beyond his wildest dreams. But God interrupts his life with the arrival of some hungry nomads from the north. The story of Joseph's reconciliation with his family fills most of the remaining chapters of Genesis 42—50, but we'll only look at selections in this study. Reading through the entire account, however, will assist you in grasping the intensity of the process. *Read Genesis 42.*

1. What emotions do you see in all the people cited in this chapter—from Jacob to Joseph to his brothers?

2. Why does Joseph throw his brothers in prison?

Why do the brothers think they are getting thrown in prison?

3. What clues does this passage give that Joseph has virtually divorced himself from his past?

In Genesis 43 and 44, the brothers—including Benjamin—visit a second time. Joseph's identity remains hidden, but he seems to toy with his brothers, asking questions about his father and entrapping Benjamin by hiding a silver cup in his bag of grain. It's all Joseph's plan to bring his father to Egypt.

4. *Read Genesis 45:1-15.* What emotions does Joseph express in this passage?

In what ways can you identify with Joseph's powerful mix of emotions?

5. What would you be feeling if you were one of the brothers?

6. Given all that has transpired in chapters 42—45, what do you learn about the process of reconciling broken relationships?

7. What does Joseph see as the purposes of his servitude, imprisonment and separation from his family?

8. How would you feel to know that all of your suffering was ultimately not just allowed by God but designed by him?

9. *Read Genesis 50:15-21.* Why do the brothers fear?

How do they deal with their fears?

10. How do you know that Joseph's forgiveness is genuine?

11. As you face the challenge of forgiving and releasing others, what do you find most challenging about the example of Joseph?

Ask God for grace to be an "aggressive forgiver"—forgiving people long before they ask.

Now or Later

Read Hebrews 12:14-15 to see what the Bible says about bitterness. What effect has bitterness had on you and on others in your life?

9

Perseverance

Acts 7:9-16;
selections from Genesis 37—50

In the opening chapter of the book of Daniel, the Bible reads, "Daniel remained there," referring to his captivity (in Babylonia, then Medo-Persia). Another translation states, "Daniel *lasted* there." He demonstrated staying power. As a slave in three empires under four kings, Daniel lasted as a godly man until he died, well into his eighties.

William Carey, the so-called father of modern missions, was asked the secret of his success in serving over forty years in India. He answered, "I can plod."

GROUP DISCUSSION. If life is a marathon, what are the day-to-day secrets of staying in and finishing the race?

PERSONAL REFLECTION. What disciplines of the spiritual life do you have the most difficulty maintaining because you don't see their impact on your daily life?

If you read the entire story of Joseph, it's easy to see his life as compressed into short bursts of serving, leading and forgiving. But Joseph's story spreads out over decades, thus teaching us something about Joseph's stick-to-it-iveness. *Read Acts 7:9-16.*

1. What are the key events in this summary of Joseph's life?

2. If you were Joseph listening to Stephen's sermon, how would you have felt as he summed up your life, hardships and achievements in these few verses?

---

3. *Read Genesis 37:2; 41:46, 53-54; 45:6.* Chart out the time line of Joseph's life. How many years transpired between Joseph's dream and the fulfillment of the first dream? (The first dream is found in Genesis 37:5-8.)

---

4. What do you think kept Joseph going through all of the years of abandonment, betrayal and forgotten dreams (Genesis 42:9)?

---

5. *Read Genesis 39:3-4, 9, 21, 23.* In these verses, what attitudes do you see in Joseph that enabled him to persevere as a servant in his younger years?

---

6. *Read Genesis 40:8; 41:16.* In these verses, what attitudes do you see in Joseph that enabled him to interpret the dreams when called on?

---

7. *Read Genesis 45:4-8; 50:15-21.* In these verses, what attitudes do you see in Joseph that enabled him to forgive in his later years?

8. Why do you think these combined attitudes gave him the resolve to persevere—even though he was not in a place that he might have chosen for himself?

9. What is the role of faith in enabling us to persevere? (See Hebrews 11:21-22.)

10. What advantage was it to Joseph to persevere?

11. What character traits do you need to be working on or asking God for now that will help you stay faithful over the years?

12. How can the Christian community help you stay faithful over the years?

Ask God to help you be a finisher in the long and challenging race ahead.

Now or Later

Do an in-depth study of the life of Daniel. Daniel 1—6 reveals a man dedicated to God, like Joseph, who served as a captive in hostile environments.

Leader's Notes

MY GRACE IS SUFFICIENT FOR YOU. *(2 COR 12:9)*

Leading a Bible discussion can be an enjoyable and rewarding experience. But it can also be *scary*—especially if you've never done it before. If this is your feeling, you're in good company. When God asked Moses to lead the Israelites out of Egypt, he replied, "O LORD, please send someone else to do it!" (Ex 4:13). It was the same with Solomon, Jeremiah and Timothy, but God helped these people in spite of their weaknesses, and he will help you as well.

You don't need to be an expert on the Bible or a trained teacher to lead a Bible discussion. The idea behind these inductive studies is that the leader guides group members to discover for themselves what the Bible has to say. This method of learning will allow group members to remember much more of what is said than a lecture would.

These studies are designed to be led easily. As a matter of fact, the flow of questions through the passage from observation to interpretation to application is so natural that you may feel that the studies lead themselves. This study guide is also flexible. You can use it with a variety of groups—student, professional, neighborhood or church groups. Each study takes forty-five to sixty minutes in a group setting.

There are some important facts to know about group dynamics and encouraging discussion. The suggestions listed below should enable you to effectively and enjoyably fulfill your role as leader.

Preparing for the Study
1. Ask God to help you understand and apply the passage in your own life. Unless this happens, you will not be prepared to lead others. Pray too for the various members of the group. Ask God to open your hearts to the message of his Word and motivate you to action.

2. Read the introduction to the entire guide to get an overview of the entire book and the issues which will be explored.

3. As you begin each study, read and reread the assigned Bible passage to familiarize yourself with it.

4. This study guide is based on the New International Version of the Bible. It will help you and the group if you use this translation as the basis for your study and discussion.

5. Carefully work through each question in the study. Spend time in meditation and reflection as you consider how to respond.

6. Write your thoughts and responses in the space provided in the study guide. This will help you to express your understanding of the passage clearly.

7. It might help to have a Bible dictionary handy. Use it to look up any unfamiliar words, names or places. (For additional help on how to study a passage, see chapter five of *How to Lead a LifeBuilder Study*, IVP, 2018.)

8. Consider how you can apply the Scripture to your life. Remember that the group will follow your lead in responding to the studies. They will not go any deeper than you do.

9. Once you have finished your own study of the passage, familiarize yourself with the leader's notes for the study you are leading. These are designed to help you in several ways. First, they tell you the purpose the study guide author had in mind when writing the study. Take time to think through how the study questions work together to accomplish that purpose. Second, the notes provide you with additional background information or suggestions on group dynamics for various questions. This information can be useful when people have difficulty understanding or answering a question. Third, the leader's notes can alert you to potential problems you may encounter during the study.

10. If you wish to remind yourself of anything mentioned in the leader's notes, make a note to yourself below that question in the study.

Leading the Study

1. Begin the study on time. Open with prayer, asking God to help the group to understand and apply the passage.

2. Be sure that everyone in your group has a study guide. Encourage the group to prepare beforehand for each discussion by reading the introduction to the guide and by working through the questions in the study.

3. At the beginning of your first time together, explain that these studies are meant to be discussions, not lectures. Encourage the members of the group to participate. However, do not put pressure on those who may be hesitant to speak during the first few sessions. You may want to suggest the following guidelines to your group.

☐ Stick to the topic being discussed.

☐ Your responses should be based on the verses which are the focus of the discussion and not on outside authorities such as commentaries or speakers.

☐ These studies focus on a particular passage of Scripture. Only rarely should you refer to other portions of the Bible. This allows for everyone to participate in in-depth study on equal ground.

☐ Anything said in the group is considered confidential and will not be discussed outside the group unless specific permission is given to do so.

☐ We will listen attentively to each other and provide time for each person present to talk.

☐ We will pray for each other.

4. Have a group member read the introduction at the beginning of the discussion.

5. Every session begins with a group discussion question. The question or activity is meant to be used before the passage is read. The question introduces the theme of the study and encourages group members to begin to open up. Encourage as many members as possible to participate, and be ready to get the discussion going with your own response.

This section is designed to reveal where our thoughts or feelings need to be transformed by Scripture. That is why it is especially important not to read the passage before the discussion question is asked. The passage will tend to color the honest reactions people would otherwise give because they are, of course, supposed to think the way the Bible does.

You may want to supplement the group discussion question with an icebreaker to help people to get comfortable. See the community section of the *Small Group Starter Kit* (IVP, 1995) for more ideas.

You also might want to use the personal reflection question with your group. Either allow a time of silence for people to respond individually or discuss it together.

6. Have a group member (or members if the passage is long) read aloud the passage to be studied. Then give people several minutes to read the passage again silently so that they can take it all in.

7. Question 1 will generally be an overview question designed to briefly survey the passage. Encourage the group to look at the whole passage, but try to avoid getting sidetracked by questions or issues that will be addressed later in the study.

8. As you ask the questions, keep in mind that they are designed to be used just as they are written. You may simply read them aloud. Or you may prefer to express them in your own words.

There may be times when it is appropriate to deviate from the study guide. For example, a question may have already been answered. If so, move on to the next question. Or someone may raise an important question not covered in the guide. Take time to discuss it, but try to keep the group from going off on tangents.

9. Avoid answering your own questions. If necessary, repeat or rephrase them until they are clearly understood. Or point out something you read in the leader's notes to clarify the context or meaning. An eager group quickly becomes passive and silent if they think the leader will do most of the talking.

10. Don't be afraid of silence. People may need time to think about the question before formulating their answers.

11. Don't be content with just one answer. Ask, "What do the rest of you think?" or "Anything else?" until several people have given answers to the question.

12. Acknowledge all contributions. Try to be affirming whenever possible. Never reject an answer. If it is clearly off-base, ask, "Which verse led you to that conclusion?" or again, "What do the rest of you think?"

13. Don't expect every answer to be addressed to you, even though this will probably happen at first. As group members become more at ease, they will begin to truly interact with each other. This is one sign of healthy discussion.

14. Don't be afraid of controversy. It can be very stimulating. If you don't resolve an issue completely, don't be frustrated. Move on and keep it in mind for later. A subsequent study may solve the problem.

15. Periodically summarize what the group has said about the passage. This helps to draw together the various ideas mentioned and gives continuity to the study. But don't preach.

16. At the end of the Bible discussion you may want to allow group members a time of quiet to work on an idea under "Now or Later." Then discuss what you experienced. Or you may want to encourage group members to work on these ideas between meetings. Give an opportunity during the session for people to talk about what they are learning.

17. Conclude your time together with conversational prayer, adapting the prayer suggestion at the end of the study to your group. Ask for God's help in following through on the commitments you've made.

18. End on time.

Many more suggestions and helps are found in *How to Lead a LifeBuilder Study.*

Components of Small Groups

A healthy small group should do more than study the Bible. There are four components to consider as you structure your time together.

Nurture. Small groups help us to grow in our knowledge and love of God. Bible study is the key to making this happen and is the foundation of your small group.

Community. Small groups are a great place to develop deep friendships with other Christians. Allow time for informal interaction before and after each study. Plan activities and games that will help you get to know each other. Spend time having fun together—going on a picnic or cooking dinner together.

Worship and prayer. Your study will be enhanced by spending time praising God together in prayer or song. Pray for each other's needs—and keep track of how God is answering prayer in your group. Ask God to help you to apply what you are learning in your study.

Outreach. Reaching out to others can be a practical way of applying what you are learning, and it will keep your group from becoming self-focused. Host a series of evangelistic discussions for your friends or neighbors. Clean up the yard of an elderly friend. Serve at a soup kitchen together, or spend a day working in the community.

Many more suggestions and helps in each of these areas are found in the *Small Group Starter Kit.* You will also find information on building a small group. Reading through the starter kit will be worth your time.

Study 1.
Building on Damaged Foundations. Genesis 29:14—30:24; 37:1-4.
Purpose: To show that our difficult backgrounds or family situations are not God's rejection of us nor are they an excuse for not growing into a productive and godly person.

General note. Throughout Genesis 37—50, Jacob (Joseph's father and the second son of Isaac [Gen 25:19ff.]) is referred to as either Jacob (his birth name) or Israel (the name God gave him in Gen 32:26-28). For the purposes of these notes, he will most often be referred to as Jacob, but his sons are identified as the twelve sons (or tribes) of Israel.

Genesis 37—50 is the account of Jacob (Israel) in that it describes the hand of God in preserving the twelve tribes of Israel and the family from which the Messiah (Jesus) will come. Genesis 37 and 39—50 focus primarily on Joseph because God uses his story to save the people of Israel (Gen 50:20). Genesis 38 diverts to a discussion on Judah and Tamar because the son that is born to them is part of the Messianic lineage (see Mt 1:3). Others suggest that Genesis 38 is designed to show Joseph as more righteous than Judah. In Genesis 38, Judah succumbs to the temptation of a prostitute; in Genesis 39, Joseph resists the temptation of Potiphar's wife.

Question 1. These verses describe Joseph's family, but the complexity, jealousies and broken relationships are described throughout the last twenty chapters of Genesis. Before the study, read the concluding remarks of Joseph's father, Jacob, in Genesis 49:1-27 to get a full picture of Joseph's family dynamics.

Questions 2-3. Allow group members to speculate outside of that which the text reveals here. The intent of this question is to get the group thinking about the relationally and emotionally dysfunctional situation out of which Joseph came.

Question 4. Joseph was the first child born to Rachel, Jacob's favorite wife, and he was born when Jacob was well advanced in years (Gen 37:3).

Question 6. Be prepared for these questions to stir up some deep hurts in people. If a group member pours her or his heart out, don't hesitate to stop and pray for that person and the needs or hurts she or he reveals.

Question 7. The text does not tell us why Joseph brings the "bad report." It's possible that Joseph was, as his father's favorite son, just a snobby tattletale who delighted in getting his brothers into trouble. It is also possible, however, that the brothers—who we'll later learn are quite adept at lying to their father—were being deceitful in their service to their father. Joseph might have filed the bad report because, in his integrity, he could not bear to see his deceptive brothers ripping off his father.

As background here, note that Jacob, the father of the clan, has a name that literally means "chiseler" or "deceiver." Earlier in the book of Genesis, he cheats his brother Esau and his father-in-law Laban by deceit and lying. As you discuss family dynamics, it might be worth asking if the sons were misbehaving on the job or if they were just imitating their conniving father?

Question 8. The beautiful coat certainly drove a wedge between the brothers and Joseph in several ways. First, it showed him as Jacob's favorite son, as the "son of his old age."

Second, the coat probably symbolized that Joseph, as his father's favorite, was exempted from physical work. The coat was a sign of nobility, and the long sleeves were an indication that Joseph was not expected to do manual work like his brothers.

Finally, the coat symbolized that Jacob had given Joseph the "mantle of authority." "The special coat provided to Joseph by his father signified a position of authority and favor" (John H. Walton and Victor H. Matthews, *The IVP Bible Background Commentary: Genesis—Deuteronomy* [Downers Grove, Ill.: InterVarsity Press, 1997], p. 70).

In terms of the birth order of the sons, the coat should have been given to Reuben, the first-born son, but Reuben had slept with his father's concubine, Bilhah (Gen 35:22). This act of deception resulted in Reuben being cursed— "you will no longer excel" (Gen 49:3-4)—and Joseph being given the birthright (according to 1 Chron 5:1-2).

The judgment on Reuben was severe because "a son who used his father's concubine was seen not only as incestuous but as attempting to usurp the authority of the family patriarch" (Walton and Matthews, *IVP Bible Background Commentary: Genesis—Deuteronomy*, p. 69).

The brothers' emotion toward this coat appears later in Genesis 37 when they strip the coat off (37:23)—perhaps expressing their rage at everything that the coat and Joseph symbolized to them.

Question 9. Remember that this was a nomadic family living in the desert. When his brothers refused to speak to Joseph, it left him in a world of social isolation.

Question 10. As you discuss this question, it might be wise to lead the group in prayer and ask God to use the life of Joseph to reassure you all that he can indeed use your lives.

Question 11. As the leader, allow people to speak honestly without rebuking them or telling them that it's never right to feel anger or disappointment toward God. In contrast, the psalmist shows his emotions often before God, and even Jesus on the cross questioned why God would let hurtful things happen to him (Mt 27:46). Recommend Philip Yancey's book *Disappointment with God* (Zondervan, 1988) for those who express strong hostility toward God for the pain of their past.

Question 12. For those who have no familiarity with what happens later in Joseph's life, this question may be unanswerable, so it might be worth giving a "Joseph-overview" before discussing question 12.

Now or Later. To help group members value this "Now or Later" idea, you should do it yourself before the study. Then you can explain the assignment personally by reading excerpts from your own journal.

Study 2. Dreams, Visions and Discretion. Genesis 37:5-11.

Purpose: To affirm the reality that God's design, dream or vision for our life may actually take us into greater hardships—all as part of his work to build and develop our character (Heb 12:5-11).

General note. As you begin this study keep in mind that many people inaugurate a relationship with God in hopes that he will solve every problem and make every difficulty disappear. This expectation has often been reinforced—especially in Western culture—by the teaching that Jesus wants to guarantee our good health and prosperity. As a result, the story of Joseph comes as an encouraging awakening to remind us that hardship often follows those who listen to God.

Question 2. The interpretations of Joseph's dreams are not very mysterious. The brothers react immediately because the interpretation is so obvious. In the ancient world, dreams were thought to offer information from the divine realm—so the brothers would have assumed that Joseph was saying to them, "Not only am I Jacob's favorite son, I'm God's favorite in the family." Encourage people to try to put themselves in the older brothers' positions (almost all of the brothers were older than Joseph, and older meant more prestigious in that culture).

Question 3. Solomon wrote, "Jealousy is as cruel as the grave" (Song 8:6 RSV). In retelling his dreams to his brothers it may seem to us that Joseph was just fanning their flame of jealousy. However, it might have been that Joseph was so troubled by the dreams that he needed to talk to someone, and they were the only ones around.

The brothers' jealousy (Gen 37:11) may also be their reaction to God in this situation because they would have seen the dreams as God speaking to

Joseph when he wasn't speaking to them. Therefore, they are angry first because he is their father's favorite, and now it seems like he's even God's favorite.

Question 4. This question has no correct answer. The purpose is to point out that Joseph was totally clueless and naive about what lay ahead.

Question 5. Joseph's dreams were certainly abnormal for a nomadic shepherd boy. Even if he were his father's favorite, there would scarcely be any context—in the present or the future—where his older brothers would have been required to bow down to their younger brother. Even if Jacob had left all of his earthly possessions to Joseph—so that the brothers would have become virtual slaves to him (in which case, dream one might have come true)—there would still never be a context where his parents would need to bow down (dream two).

Perhaps the source of the dream was not just the random act of the Spirit of God but instead a sovereign foreshadowing of God acting through the action of Jacob. The favorite-son coat that Jacob had given him could have put dreams of royalty into Joseph's head. However, Jacob saw the dreams more pensively because Jacob himself had had his life transformed by dreams from heaven (see Gen 28:10-22; 32:22-32).

Question 6. Because Joseph's dreams and the revelation of these dreams to the other players in the dreams seem self-serving and even prideful, it is reasonable to assume that his brothers thought his favorite-son status had gone to his head. Were his dreams of God or from his ego—or both? God's interaction with our mixed motives might be a good discussion topic here—but don't get too far off track.

Questions 7-8. Many are not familiar with the experience of God speaking through dreams and visions. For the purpose of this study, however, you don't need to belabor the "hows" of supernatural dreams. Instead you can expand the definition of dreams and visions to include things like "your dream for your life" or "what you think is God's will for your life" or "your sense of God-given destiny."

Question 9. The most important thing to point out in this discussion is that God's work through dreams, impressions and visions can come from multiple sources. He can intervene by putting supernatural thoughts into our minds, as in Acts 16:9. Or he can speak through our psyche in response to the emotions and fears related to situations around us, as seen in Matthew 1:19-20 and Acts 10:1-43. God works through the whole of our lives. For Joseph, his relationships, age, daydreams and the supernatural action of God were all part of God's work to give him these dreams.

Question 10. Freely alter this question according to the age of the people in the group. In other words, if the group members are nineteen years old, then go back to age ten or twelve. If the group is all over age fifty, go back to age twenty-five or thirty. The intent of the question is to explore what God might have been saying to people when they were younger and perhaps less encumbered by their current worries.

Now or Later. Encourage the group to do this by reading Ephesians 3:20-21 and asking, "What dreams or visions or life goals do you have that only God can accomplish?"

Study 3. Leaving Your Dream with God. Genesis 37:12-36.

Purpose: To find encouragement to stay faithful to God, even when our dreams have not been fulfilled and prayers have not been answered in the ways we hoped.

General note. As the entirety of this nine-part study will show, Joseph's life is about maintaining integrity even when life turns difficult, dreams are dashed, people betray you and everything turns out different than what you expected. This study shows us the first major twist that God brings into Joseph's life road.

Question 1. Joseph was no longer out doing the work of shepherding alongside his brothers. He was at home being his father's favorite while his brothers were out doing the work—a fact that certainly aggravated the brothers.

Throughout the narrative of the family of Jacob, Jacob is presented as a very passive and weak father. In this passage, rather than going to see his sons, he sends Joseph in his stead. Jacob's example of being a father could lead your group into discussion about ways that parents can do children harm by being passive and uninvolved in their lives.

Question 3. Lead the group into discussion about the impact of bitterness on our perspectives (stereotyping) and on our ability to relate to others (hatred, anger and lying). Invite someone to look up verses related to bitterness (Prov 14:10; Eph 4:31; Heb 12:15). Read these verses to enlarge the discussion and examine the consequences.

Question 4. God uses Reuben's response and the brothers' inability to agree on what should be done with Joseph to preserve his life.

The cistern also allowed the brothers to hold Joseph without drowning him: "Cisterns were hollowed out of the limestone bedrock or were dug and then lined with plaster to store water. They provided water for humans and animals through most of the dry months. When they were empty, they sometimes served as temporary cells for prisoners (see Jeremiah 38:6)" (Walton and Matthews, *IVP Bible Background Commentary: Genesis—Deuteronomy*, pp. 70-71).

Question 5. In spite of the fact that Reuben had been bypassed (because of his past sin with his father's concubine) as the first-born deserving the coat-of-privilege, he still saw himself as the protector of his younger brothers, especially his father's favorites—Joseph here and Benjamin later (Gen 42:37).

It is also very possible that Reuben saw the rescue of Joseph as a potential bridge to heal his broken relationship with his father.

Question 6. Joseph's silence does not mean that he had no emotions. He probably experienced: fear—wondering if he would survive; regret—for the brokenness in his relationships with his brothers; surprise—in his naiveté, he probably did not realize how much they hated him; panic—his most probable prayer was "God help me!"

Question 7. The brothers divide and cannot agree on how to execute their anger. Reuben is ignored—so much so that he will later blame the family problems on the brothers with an "I told you so" discourse (Gen 42:22). And they unintentionally further the gulf between themselves and their father by planning ahead to deceive him with their story of how Joseph disappeared. Their bitterness is evident in their action against the symbol of their hatred—the coat. They strip him of it (Gen 37:23), and they incorporate it into their lie to their father (Gen 37:31-33).

At this juncture, we know little on how this action affects the brothers' relationships with God. Much later, we discover that they knew God was angry with their action, because they attribute their difficulties to God's punishment (see Gen 42:21-22).

Question 8. Jacob incurs a double loss: he has lost the first-born son of his favorite wife, Rachel, who is now deceased (Gen 35:16-21). He grieves because there is no way to replace those whom he has lost.

Question 9. If you have group members who are skilled in role-playing, this question can come alive if you have one member play Joseph and another play God—while a third reads through the events that transpired in this chapter.

Question 10. Identify the brothers' actions—stereotyping, hatred, lying—as a byproduct of their bitterness and then transition into discussing the bitterness that people can feel toward those closest to them. You might give group members a few minutes to reflect quietly on this question and write personal prayers to God about the bitterness they are struggling with.

Questions 11-12. Conclude the study by inviting discussion on patience and the concept of "waiting on God"—especially in the context of waiting on God when he has allowed circumstances into your life that seemingly contradict the dreams that you believe he has given you.

Study 4. Sexual Purity: When All Else Fails—Run! Genesis 39:6-20.

Purpose: To demonstrate that character—in this case, tested by moral temptation—is ultimately lived out in our daily choices, especially the choices that no one sees except God.

General note. This account of the life of Joseph has been paralleled with the life of Christ as described in Matthew 4. In each case, before Joseph's or Jesus' greatest impact was felt, there was a test, a temptation that had to be passed. The biblical equation is clear: testing and temptation often precede character development and maximum usefulness to God. Romans 5:1-5 links suffering to character and hope. James 1:2-4 links testing with perseverance and maturity. Joseph's story connects testing with living a life of integrity before the God who is always with us.

Question 1. Outside of the dialogue between Jesus and Satan in his great temptations (Mt 4:1-11), the story of Joseph and this woman is perhaps the most vivid and detailed story of temptation and resisting temptation in the Bible.

The writer starts with a blunt description of Joseph's physique and good looks. This attention to specifics is most likely included to underscore the fact that this was a legitimate temptation for Joseph. This type of physical description in the Bible is given four times—here and describing David, Solomon and Absalom.

The reader might logically ask, "But wouldn't Potiphar have been a man much older than Joseph, and therefore his wife as well, thus making this older woman easier for Joseph to resist?" In that culture, a man of Potiphar's stature could have had many wives, and when he tired of older ones, he married a younger one. Thus, it is likely that Joseph and Potiphar's wife were close in age; she may have actually been younger than Joseph.

Question 2. The description of Joseph as "well built and handsome" (NASB) probably indicates that Potiphar's wife's attraction to him was motivated by physical lust and desire. Perhaps Potiphar, the older man, was no longer muscular and handsome, and perhaps his virility was waning.

Potiphar's wife may also have been motivated by rebellion. In that culture, she was little better than a slave to her husband, so flirting with the chief of the household was a way to get back at Potiphar, her master.

Two other factors that may have provoked Potiphar's wife's attempted seduction include: she might have been bored and looking for excitement; and she could have been a trap placed by Satan in an effort to derail Joseph and thus prevent his role in saving the tribes of Israel.

Question 3. Joseph had several good reasons to rationalize saying yes to her advances: she was probably beautiful; he could rationalize that God had sent her to help him deal with his loneliness; he could have concluded that no one would ever find out; he might have thought, "She's powerful and connected in high places—she could help me get my dreams fulfilled."

Question 6. Joseph's reasons for resistance included loyalty to his master, but his question in Genesis 39:6 reveals that he was living his life before God as his "audience of one." Note that he didn't say, "How could I do this thing and sin against Potiphar," nor "How could I do this thing and sin against you?" His moral character was motivated by his relationship with God: "How could I do this wicked thing and sin *against God?*"

Some commentators speculate that Joseph was exceedingly cautious in this area because he had seen the damage Reuben's immorality had brought on him when he pursued his father's concubine (see Gen 35:22 and 49:3-4).

Question 7. When the situation intensified, Joseph ran (Gen 39:13). We don't know whether Joseph walked into the house knowing that she had cleared everyone out or not. We do know that when she confronted him with the hottest enticement, he was close enough to her for her to grab his garment. And when she did, Joseph stopped resisting verbally. He ran out of the house and left the garment behind.

Several other things to note with regard to Joseph's resistance: first, note again that Joseph's garment symbolizes his life. "Besides the interesting parallel to Joseph's brothers' taking his cloak, it should be noted here again the cloak is to serve to identify Joseph" (Walton and Matthews, *IVP Bible Background Commentary: Genesis—Deuteronomy*, p. 74).

Second, Joseph's strength in the face of temptation led Mohammed to set him forth as an example in the Koran. Sura 12 features Joseph's resistance and running. Potiphar's wife trapped him in the house by bolting the doors (Sura 12:23), but he ran. "And they raced with one another to the door, and she tore his shirt from behind" (Sura 12:25). Mohammed emphasized the fact that Joseph was running and she was trying to catch him. In the Koran, Joseph used the shirt torn from behind in his defense (Sura 12:26, 27).

Other stories like Joseph and Potiphar's wife exist and may simply be another rendering of this same story or a carryover later in history: "The Nineteenth Dynasty (c. 1225 B.C.) Egyptian tale of Anubis and Bata has many similarities to the story of Joseph and Potiphar's wife" (Walton and Matthews, *IVP Bible Background Commentary: Genesis—Deuteronomy*, p. 73).

Questions 9 and 12. Joseph's obedient action before God and the subsequent consequences (he goes to prison under false charges) serve as the biblical reminder that sometimes obedience is not rewarded. Jesus obeyed God to the utmost, and he ended up on the cross.

Spend some time on this issue because group members need to know that acting out of character and integrity can sometimes be costly. Invite people to share experiences of making the right, moral choice yet suffering bad or tough consequences.

Question 10. Scholars note that Potiphar's position, as captain of the pharaoh's guard, would have made him also the chief executioner. As a result, he could have served as judge, jury and executioner in Joseph's case. And Joseph, as a slave without rights, was defenseless before his accuser. Add to this the fact that Potiphar's wife had made sure that there was no one in the house to observe the interchange, who could then object to her accusation or defend Joseph, and you would fully expect that Joseph would have been executed.

The probable reason that Potiphar did not have Joseph put to death was that he did not believe his wife. Perhaps he knew her to be a liar or he knew Joseph to be a man of character—or both—but Joseph was not killed. Instead, probably to save face, Potiphar imprisoned Joseph. This action set the stage for the next chapter in Joseph's story: "Rather than being executed for rape (as dictated in, for instance, the Middle Assyrian laws), Joseph was put into a royal prison holding political prisoners. This may have been a bit more comfortable (as prisons go), but more importantly, it will put him in contact with members of Pharaoh's court" (Walton and Matthews, *IVP Bible Background Commentary: Genesis—Deuteronomy,* p. 74).

Question 11. When the temptation gets too heated, run! Dietrich Bonhoeffer described temptation vividly in this account:

> In our members there is a slumbering inclination towards desire which is both sudden and fierce. With irresistible power desire seizes mastery over the flesh. All at once a secret, smoldering fire is kindled. The flesh burns and is in flames. It makes no difference whether it is sexual desire, or ambition, or vanity, or desire for revenge, or love of fame and power, or greed for money, or, finally, that strange desire for the beauty of the world, of nature. Joy in God is in course of being extinguished in us and we seek all our joy in the creature. At this moment God is quite unreal to us, he loses all reality and only desire for the creature is real; the only reality is the devil. Satan does not here fill us with hatred of God, but with forgetfulness of God. . . . The lust thus aroused envelops the mind and will of man in deepest darkness. *The powers of discrimination and of decision are taken from us.* . . . It is here that everything within me rises up against the Word of God. (*Temptation* [New York: Macmillan, 1953], pp. 116-17)

Now or Later. Proverbs 7:6-27 shows us another young man who, unlike Joseph, did not run from temptation. Instead, he walked right into it "like an ox to the slaughter" or "like a bird rushing into a snare." This account in Proverbs, probably written autobiographically by Solomon, describes the destruction wrought in his own life because of his inability to resist sexual temptation.

Study 5. The Integrity of a Servant. Genesis 39:1-6, 20-23.

Purpose: To find encouragement to be obedient servants, even when we find ourselves in situations that we would never choose.

General note. The Bible is full of stories about the people of God living in adverse circumstances. Here we find Joseph in prison. Later in the Old Testament, we will find God's people in captivity or exile. Esther was a captive taken into the king's harem, and Daniel and his three friends were prisoners in Babylon.

In the New Testament, the story continues and adversity abounds—from the rejection and crucifixion of Jesus, to the martyrdom of Steven, the imprisonment of the apostles and the prison epistles of the apostle Paul.

If we define prison as "any undesirable circumstance that we find ourselves in that we would never choose and from which we'd like to be released," the Bible has much to say to us. Joseph's example teaches about the grace of God for God's people while facing adversity.

Question 1. For Joseph, everything in Egypt would have been foreign. He had been launched from the life of a desert nomad into the household of the rich and powerful Potiphar. Changes that Joseph faced included: language, attire, customs, foods, religion. Add to this the conflicting emotions that Joseph brought with him into Egypt. Try to get the group to articulate the varying emotions he must have experienced—from homesickness to anger to bitterness to confusion.

Questions 2-3. When the text says that "the Lord caused all that [Joseph] did to prosper in his hands," it most likely refers to economic and agricultural prosperity. Verse 6 identifies the prosperity as "in house and field"—so we can assume that under Joseph's leadership, the fields were better managed and therefore increased the harvest. Perhaps the management of the household finances was more efficient so that Potiphar saw himself getting richer. If there were livestock, the prosperity would have been measured both by the reproduction rates and by the output of things like milk, wool or meat.

Depending on the background of the group members, it may be worth taking time to discuss what "prosperity" means for the follower of Jesus Christ. The popularity (at least in the United States) of books like *The Prayer of Jabez* indicates that prosperity is being viewed in material terms. If God is with us, will our finances increase and our businesses get more successful and our families be blessed? Allow this discussion without feeling compelled to arrive at an answer—but try to provoke people to ask the question.

Use the responses to question 3 as a reminder that God does not *always* act in some formulaic fashion. Sometimes we're obedient, and we go to prison (or to the cross in the case of the most successful person who ever lived!). Other times the results of obedience include material prosperity and opportunities to lead—as with Joseph in Potiphar's house and, later, Joseph in prison.

Question 4. In leading the discussion about being "successful" and God's definition of success, it helps to refer the group to Psalm 1. These verses outline success in God's eyes.

One of the largest areas of Joseph's success was his apparent victory over his attitude. As the group identifies how they might have felt during all of these changes and disappointments and betrayals, point out that Joseph—at least as he is recorded in these chapters—never resorts to self-pity or whining.

A helpful illustration used to describe Joseph refers to him as a "thermostat" person rather than a "thermometer" person. The latter can tell you the temperature, complain about their environment and long for change, but the former seeks to change the temperature. Joseph went from being his father's favorite son to being an obscure slave and later a prisoner—but through it all he remained committed to changing his environments rather than being beaten down by them.

Question 5. In prison, Joseph distinguished himself as he did when he was a slave in Potiphar's house: his character stood out above the other people around him, and his master noticed. There was something in his countenance or his attitude or his demeanor in doing the undesirable tasks that set him apart and led the masters to conclude that this was a special young man.

In both situations, the master promoted Joseph to being his executive director of all his affairs. Genesis 39:5 notes that Joseph was overseer of Potiphar's house, in charge of everything (Gen 39:6). In the prison, Joseph became the caretaker of all prisoners (Gen 39:22) and the one who ran the prison. These promotions foreshadow Joseph's ultimate destiny because the language will be repeated when Joseph gets promoted to the service of Pharaoh and is put in charge of all of Egypt (Gen 41:37-45).

Question 6. This is a speculative question, but it must be noted that this is the royal prison (Gen 39:20)—the Egyptian equivalent of our prisons for "white collar" criminals. Joseph's distinguishing service could have included leading the other prisoners in their assigned tasks, keeping the prison clean or lifting the sagging morale of the other prisoners. The word *care* in Genesis 39:22 could imply that Joseph became the chaplain or pastor of the prison, a role that will be evident when he cares for the cupbearer and the baker in Genesis 40.

Question 8. The phrase "the LORD was with Joseph" signifies several realities concerning Joseph's relationship to God and to his work. There was productivity in Potiphar's house (Gen 39:2-6), and perhaps there was increased order in the prison—so much so that the captain of the guard no longer needed to "pay heed" to the things Joseph did (Gen 39:21, 23).

This phrase also carries three significant meanings or implications. First, it describes Joseph's demeanor. There was a confidence or a serving attitude that set him apart from others. Joseph—to use New Testament language—was a "light of the world" person in some very dark environs, and people took notice.

Second, it describes Joseph's relationship with God. Joseph had a consciousness of God's presence that helped him rise above his circumstances. This awareness of his living and vital relationship before the presence of God is what gave him strength to resist the temptation of Potiphar's wife (Gen 3:9).

Finally, the phrase the "the LORD was with Joseph" describes something supernatural. The spirit of God was on Joseph, and as a result, he was living out his life with God's power enabling him to rise to each new challenge.

Question 9. Encourage people to think very practically here so that the discussion does not become exclusively cerebral. Rephrasing the question can help. For example, read Matthew 5:13-16 aloud and ask, "In our day to day relationships and responsibilities, what sets us apart as the 'light' and 'salt' of Jesus?"

Question 10. These questions may provoke some more discussion about being a "thermostat" person versus a "thermometer" person. Invite discussion about the issue of *choosing* our attitudes, *choosing* to serve, *choosing* not to complain.

The story of Viktor Frankl can add to the discussion. Viktor Frankl became a famous psychiatrist as a result of his studies of fellow prisoners in a Nazi concentration camp during World War II. He studied why some died and others survived, and he arrived at one basic theme: *attitude.* He wrote of those that walked through the concentration camp huts "comforting others, giving away their last piece of bread." Then he concluded, "They may have been few in number, but they offer proof that everything can be taken from a man but one thing: the last of the human freedoms—to choose one's attitudes in any given set of circumstances" (quoted in Gordon MacDonald, *Rediscovering Yourself* [Holland, Mich.: Revell, 1985], p. 209).

The words *pit* (Gen 37:19, 22, 24) and *dungeon* (Gen 40:15) are similar. Joseph spent significant time in very undesirable circumstances, but—as we find out later—God will use the "pit" in the development of his character.

Invite people to share their experiences of staying faithful through life's pits. Ask them to be specific in describing *how* they found the strength to keep on serving—even when they were not sure why God had them there.

Now or Later. The book of Philippians, one of Paul the apostle's last letters, is written from captivity, yet it is characterized by the word *joy.* The word *joy* or *rejoice* appears fourteen times in four chapters. Encourage group members to read through this book and look for parallels between Paul's attitudes and Joseph's. Specifically, encourage them to compare Joseph and Paul in order to see how happiness—an emotion dependent on the "happenings" or circumstances of life—is different than joy.

Study 6. Discernment. Genesis 40:1—41:32.

Purpose: To demonstrate that the person of integrity will often have the opportunity to speak into the lives of others—which includes both good news and bad news.

General note. Dreams and their interpretations play a very significant role in the Bible and specifically in the lives of the characters in the book of Genesis. God preserves Sarah, Abraham's wife through a dream that warned King Abimelech (Gen 20:3, 6). Jacob's life is marked by the dream that showed him the ladder into heaven (Gen 28:10-15). Other dreams (Gen 31:10-11) as well as encounters with God (Gen 32:22ff) made Jacob sensitive to the intervention of God through the miraculous, and thus more pensive about Joseph's dream (Gen 37:11).

Joseph's life is about dreams—both his own and of those around him: the cupbearer, the baker and the pharaoh. His ability with interpreting the messages of God reveals that Joseph listened to the spirit of God who in turn made him wise and discerning.

Question 1. The king of Egypt (who will also be referred to as Pharaoh) is angry; we don't know why, but the fact that the two who go to prison are the cupbearer and the baker implies that he was dissatisfied with something related to a feast. The pharaoh was absolutely powerful, so if his wine was bitter or his toast was burnt, he could send these men to prison. And, with a snap of the fingers, he could have them executed.

The cupbearer was Pharaoh's confidant and sat with Pharaoh throughout the day. The chief baker worked for the cupbearer (thus the phrase, "his baker," in Gen 40:1). The way the story turns out probably indicates that these two were imprisoned for a culinary mistake—and they're placed in prison until fault is assigned to one or the other.

Both of these men entered prison terrified because they knew the power of the king to execute them at a whim. They both have dreams that they cannot figure out, and they are "troubled" (Gen 40:6) and visibly distressed (Gen 40:8). A dream was seen as a message from the spirit world, but if it went uninterpreted, the dreamer had no recourse but to worry that it meant bad news.

In that context, Joseph went as a servant. He observed their distress and offered himself as the discerning voice of God.

Question 3. If people have trouble answering this, ask them to consider what they know about Joseph's own past experiences with dreams.

There are two things to note about Joseph's offer to hear the dreams and explain them. First, he offered himself, but he acknowledged absolute dependency on God (Gen 40:8). Second, he offered himself and confidently asserted that God was the interpreter of dreams, yet to the best of our knowledge, Joseph lived with the daily reminder that he had dreams of his own that were uninterpreted and unfulfilled.

Question 4. People of that day often saw their dreams as bad omens and as warnings from the netherworld. Thus, the cupbearer's positive interpretation from Joseph gave the baker confidence that his dream's meaning was likewise positive. The translation of the dream dashed these hopes.

Question 5. These verses provide one of the very few glimpses of Joseph's perspective of his circumstances. He asked the cupbearer to show him kindness and speak on behalf of his unjust imprisonment. He recounted his story of being "stolen" from the land of the Hebrews.

The wording of Genesis 40:14 reflects a bit of desperation. The wording is an urgent plea: "Get me out of here!" No one was closer to the Pharaoh than the chief cupbearer, and Joseph knew that if the cupbearer represented him favorably to Pharaoh, his chances of being released increased dramatically.

Question 6. In the Hebrew Bible, repeating a phrase was a way of emphasizing its intensity (note that both Joseph's and Pharaoh's dreams come in repeated pairs). This twofold emphasis occurs in Genesis 40:23; the summary underscores the disappointment that Joseph must have felt, because the phrase is repeated—he *did not remember him*; he *forgot him*. Joseph could have sunk into despair because he knew, as the days after the cupbearer's release lengthened, that his request had been ignored. He was stuck in prison.

Question 7. It is interesting to note that Genesis 41:1 emphasizes the reality of how Joseph was forgotten in the use of the word *full,* saying, "When two full years had passed"—reminding the reader of Joseph's endurance.

Question 8. In Genesis 41:16, Joseph reiterates his earlier statement (Gen 40:8) that the interpretation of dreams belongs to God. As the voice of God, Joseph promised Pharaoh "God's peace." (shalom: Gen 41:16). The reality that "the Lord was with Joseph" played out again in Joseph's ability to discern the messages that God was sending through these dreams.

Question 9. The cupbearer did more than just test wines and other beverages. He served as Pharaoh's right-hand man and his constant attendant. Thus, when Joseph stood before Pharaoh, the cupbearer—whom Joseph had served in prison and who had forgotten Joseph for two full years—would have been standing there beside him. The miraculous ability of Joseph to forgive those who had hurt him manifests itself here as he maintained silence toward the cupbearer.

Question 10. Joseph's interpretation of the baker's dream (Gen 40:16-19) illustrated that Joseph was willing to bring good news and bad news. He saw himself only as the mouthpiece of God, delivering the interpretation that the spirit of God gave him. To tell Pharaoh—who could execute a man for burning his toast—that seven years of famine and hardship were coming might have created a desire in Joseph to soften his message, but Joseph never backed down.

Questions 11-12. The intent of these questions is to provoke the discussion, "Why are we not more like Joseph?" which will hopefully lead group members to consider Joseph as a model to emulate. His dependency on God, his belief that God was with him, his faith and his confidence that God was speaking all provide exemplary traits for us to imitate.

Now or Later. Discernment is a biblically desirable trait that is often ignored in our contemporary teaching on Christian growth. Hebrews 5:14 emphasizes the role of experience, practice and even mistakes as God's tools to help us discern good versus evil. Emphasize to the group that discernment is a skill and trait learned over time, as the combination of life experience, the work of the Holy Spirit and the knowledge of the Word of God work together to help us grow in wisdom.

Study 7. Long-Range Planning. Genesis 41:33-57.

Purpose: To demonstrate that the life of integrity and character functions with a long-term view—both in terms of planning ahead and in terms of seeing God's long-term purposes.

General note. One of the great themes of Scripture is that God is moving through human history toward the achievement of his will and purposes. Joseph's story now slowly moves him into a position of power where he will be used of God to save not only the people of Egypt but also the twelve tribes of Israel and, in the long-term purposes of God, the lineage of the Messiah.

Question 1. Joseph lets Pharaoh know that he has a plan. It's easy to see how the management of Potiphar's house and then the coordination of the prison have developed Joseph's giftedness as an organizer. This point should also be reviewed in question 7 (below).

Question 2. Genesis 41:33 certainly comes across as Joseph's initiative in promoting himself before Pharaoh, but Joseph is a man with a mission of leadership. He rose to the top in Potiphar's house, in the prison and now before Pharaoh. Joseph had already lobbied the cupbearer and asked him to speak on Joseph's behalf—but he forgot him. Joseph now speaks for himself.

As the group discusses Joseph's boldness in putting himself forward, discuss the role of divinely given self-confidence versus self-serving pride. Joseph certainly illustrates that being a man or woman of God does not mean that we need to retire sheepishly. Instead, with God-given confidence, we can say with boldness, "I am the person to face this challenge."

Question 3. Leaders of that day were seen as divinities and those who entered their presence went in with fear. The biblical account of Esther recounts that entering the presence of a ruler uninvited could result in death (Esther 4:11). Pharaoh was so powerful that most of the people around him would have concentrated more on trying to please him rather than on speaking boldly to him. But Joseph went with an assurance that "the LORD was with him," and he set himself apart from all others by being bold, by putting himself forward and by confidently suggesting a plan.

Question 4. The signet ring, as well as the chariot, helps us understand the absolute power that was given to Joseph that day. Pharaoh delegates power to Joseph (Gen 41:41) and then gives him the ring.

Others add to the description of the power Joseph now wielded: "Kings and royal administrators used a signet ring to seal official documents. This ring would have been distinctive and would have contained the name (cartouche in Egypt) of the king. Anyone using it acted in the name of the king (see Num 31:50; Esther 3:10; Tobit 1:20; 1 Maccabees 6:15)" (Walton and Matthews, *IVP Bible Background Commentary: Genesis—Deuteronomy*, p. 76).

One of the traits of Joseph's depth of character was his ability to change environments without himself being changed. As you discuss these transitions, consider recounting the amazing life of South African Nelson Mandela, who, like Joseph, walked out of decades of prison into national leadership and eventually the presidency of his country.

Question 5. After years in Egypt, it's reasonable to assume that Joseph had abandoned all hope of seeing his family again or returning to the land of the Hebrews. So why would he commit to working hard for his pagan boss and serving the people of Egypt?

The secret of Joseph's motivation takes us back to Genesis 39. Joseph believed that his work was ultimately done before God. He exemplified the fact that all that we do is work offered up to God. Colossians 3:22-24 adds to this discussion and serves as a summary of Joseph's work habits.

Joseph's example, however, is not without some problems. The name and the wife he received from Pharaoh (Gen 41:45) open the question, "To what extent do we identify with the pagan culture around us?" When he accepted this wife and this name, the text tells us that he gained authority over the land.

Was he compromising? Consider the following: Joseph was given a new name. Pharaoh chose this, naming him Zaphenath-Paneah. This name carries significance. In the heart of it is the syllable *nath*. Nath was one of the goddesses of Egypt. Thus, Joseph's new name meant, "The god speaks and lives"! Pharaoh wanted Joseph incorporated into the Egyptian religious worldview.

He was also given a wife that identified him with the religion and culture of Egypt. Her name was Asenath. Again, notice that syllable *nath*. His wife's name meant "belonging to Nath," and she was a daughter of an Egyptian priest

Question 6. The chronology of Joseph's life will be the topic of study 9, so it's best not to spend too much time on this detail. All that should be observed is that Joseph was thirty years old (Gen 41:36) as he entered the service of Pharaoh. It had been two years since he helped the cupbearer (Gen 41:1) and thirteen years since he dreamed his dream (Gen 37:2).

Joseph's motivation can only be attributed to his desire to serve his God—no matter where he found himself.

Question 7. See question 1 above.

Question 8. As the famine commences, Joseph's forethought and planning move him from leadership and influence in Egypt to leadership and influence in the world. Note how amazing this is, from slave to prisoner to second most

powerful person in that part of the world—all in two decades.
Question 9. The naming of Joseph's sons reveals his inmost feeling about the past (Gen 41:51-52). "There was still something missing . . . he had not forgotten his father's household" (G. J. Wenham, ed., *New Bible Commentary*, rev. ed. [Downers Grove, Ill.: InterVarsity Press, 1994], p. 87).
Question 11. Encourage group members to share their dreams of what they hope God will do in and through their lives. Then invite discussion by asking: "Should you work and plan to make these dreams occur or just accept whatever God brings along?"
Now or Later. The book of Proverbs refers extensively to the idea of planning. Instruct the group that if they pursue this, to note the creative tension in the book of Proverbs with the issue of planning and the frequent reaffirmation of the sovereignty of God.

Study 8. Forgiveness and Release. Genesis 42; 45:1-15; 50:15-21.
Purpose: To put Joseph forward as an example of releasing his bitterness toward those who betrayed him and giving them—and himself—a fresh start.
General note. The texts covered in this study reveal the multiple emotions that Joseph and his family encountered as they moved toward forgiveness and reconciliation. The story of Joseph's reconciliation with his family fills most of the remaining chapters of Genesis 42—50; this study looks only at selections. As leader, you will benefit by reading through the entire account in order to assist you in grasping the intensity of the process.
Personal reflection. The personal reflection question and the questions that follow may open up a host of emotions. Go into this study prayerfully because the Spirit of God may powerfully work to initiate the process of group members taking steps toward relational reconciliation.
Question 1. Jacob illustrates that things are probably not smooth at home; his outburst (Gen 42:1) demonstrates *anger and impatience* with lazy sons.

Joseph saw and recognized his brothers, but given his Egyptian haircut, makeup, language and dress—plus the impact of over twenty years of aging—his brothers didn't recognize him. Joseph's first emotion was *repulsion* as he failed to identify himself. There's good reason to assume that Joseph was overwhelmed with emotions like *regret* and *nostalgia* for home as his dream came back to mind.

The brothers' emotions ranged from *humiliation* because they were acknowledging their need to these Egyptian foreigners. Then there was *fear* when Joseph accused them of being spies (Gen 42:9-20); they knew that Joseph could have had them instantly killed. Later the brothers expressed the emotion of *regret* (Gen 42:21), and Reuben resorted to *blaming* (Gen 42:22).

Joseph heard and understood the entire dialogue, and his pent up emotions of twenty years or more provoked *weeping* (Gen 42:24).

Further *fear* arose when they found that their silver had been returned (Gen 42:27-28) and *confusion* as they recounted the story to their father, Jacob (Gen 42:29-34). Finally, the chapter concludes with Reuben's offer of his own sons—which may have been an expression of a *desperate desire to win his father's love* (Gen 42:37)—followed by Jacob imagining the worst as he *grieved* over the possibility of losing his other favorite son, the second son of Rachel, Benjamin (Gen 42:38).

Question 2. While the Bible doesn't tell us why he put his brothers in prison, the most logical assumption is that their appearance had confused Joseph emotionally. He gave himself three days to quiet his emotions and determine his course of action with them. The brothers' only understanding as to why they got thrown in prison is the accusation of spying, a crime deserving death.

In Genesis 42:21, commentators point out that the brothers' confession and regret is the only acknowledgment of sin in Genesis.

Question 3. Joseph had been away from his family for over twenty years (he was seventeen when he was sold into slavery, thirty when he entered the service of Pharaoh; there were seven years of plenty, and he is into the years of famine). He had forgotten them, a fact illustrated by his reaction when his brothers showed up—"Joseph also remembered the dreams he had dreamed about them" (Gen 42:9).

Pause and ask the group, "If Joseph's dream was not keeping him going, what do you think was?"

Miroslav Volf looks to the naming of Joseph's sons to illustrate his complicated relationship with his past, a past that now stood before him as his brothers returned to his life:

> Joseph was ready to undertake the difficult journey of reconciliation with his brothers who sold him into slavery because, as he put it, "God has made me forget all my hardship and all my father's house" (41:51). Before coming to an end, the journey of reconciliation entailed a good deal of remembering, however. Joseph himself was reminded of the suffering his brothers had caused, and subtly but powerfully he made them remember it too (42:21-23; 44:27ff.). Yet, like the distant light of a place called home, the divine gift of forgetting what he still remembered—"backgrounding" the memory might be the right term—guided the whole journey of return. Wanting to insure that the precious gift be lost neither on him nor on his posterity, Joseph inscribed it into the name of his son, Manasseh—"one who causes to be forgotten." A paradoxical memorial to forgetting (how can one be reminded to forget without being reminded of what one should forget?), Manasseh's presence recalled the suffering in order to draw attention to the loss of its memory. It is this strange forgetting, still interspersed with indispens-

able remembering, that made Joseph, the victim, able to embrace his brothers, the perpetrators (45:14-15)—and become theirs and his own savior (46:1ff). (Miroslav Volf, *Exclusion and Embrace* [Nashville: Abingdon, 1996], p. 139)

Questions 4-5. The "cat and mouse" game over, Joseph exploded with emotion and made himself known to the brothers. The brothers were probably stunned beyond belief, thus making it necessary for Joseph to repeat the proclamation twice (Gen 45:3 and 45:4). The brothers—at least the ten who had sold him into slavery—must have been paralyzed with fear: "What will he do to us?"

But as Joseph described their future, they probably were pinching themselves to see if they were awake. Like Joseph's journey from prisoner to second-in-command of Egypt in one day, this interchange launched the brothers from nomadic beggars from the north to the distinguished guests of the second most powerful man in Egypt.

Question 6. The story of Joseph's reunion with his brothers flows with emotions—fear, anger, weeping, confusion. The basic message? Reconciliation is a messy, inexact process!

Question 7. In the time between the brothers' first visit and their second, Joseph must have spent some time trying to evaluate the purpose of God for his years in Egypt. He articulates his perspective in Genesis 45:7-8.

Question 8. Joseph's recounting of his perceptions of God's purposes in all of his suffering invite discussion of the concept of theodicy—the role of God in evil. Did God allow this suffering in Joseph's life or did he design it? The Hebrew mindset saw God as ultimately the source of all that occurs in one's life. If good things happened, it came from God. If bad things happened, these came from God too. Job reflects this worldview when he attributes his losses to the hand of God (Job 1:21) and asks his wife, "Shall we receive the good at the hand of God and not receive the bad?" (Job 2:10). Job finally resolves to stay faithful even if God kills him (Job 13:15). Isaiah reflects the same perspective with the attribution both of light and darkness, weal and woe, to God (Is 45:7). Jeremiah, facing incredible hardship, asks, "Is it not from the mouth of the Most High that good and bad come?" (Lam 3:38).

Question 9. After their father died, the brothers feared that Joseph would now exact his revenge on them.

Lying is unfortunately part of the heritage of the children of Abraham. Abraham (when he was still called Abram) lied about Sarah (Gen 12:11-13). Isaac lied about Rebekah (Gen 26:7-10), and Jacob's (the deceiver) life was built on lies (Gen 25:29-34; 27:5-30).

When the brothers felt under pressure before Joseph, like their father, grandfather and great-grandfather, they lied. They put words in Jacob's mouth to save their own skin. We have no record of Jacob ever stating the words they repeated in Genesis 50:16-17.

Question 10. Joseph spoke peace to his brothers. A second time he reaffirmed the sovereign hand of God in all of their doings, and the forgiveness was completed.

Question 11. Joseph's apparent ability to release those who hurt him puts Joseph into a class of his own in terms of Christlike grace. Anne Lamott writes, "Forgiveness is giving up all hope of having had a different past" (*Traveling Mercies* [New York: Pantheon, 1999], p. 213). Joseph had let go of that hope. He had accepted his past and had moved on.

Now or Later. When introducing Hebrews 12:14-15, remind the group that bitterness and an unforgiving spirit affects not only the parties involved but also the communities to which we belong.

Study 9. Perseverance. Acts 7:9-16; selections from Genesis 37—50.

Purpose: To encourage faithful endurance in following God toward his purposes for our lives.

General note. "Finishing the race" is a major theme in the Bible, especially in the New Testament. The book of Hebrews was written primarily to encourage people not to quit their faith (see Heb 12:1-3). The book of Revelation came to early Christians as an encouragement to persevere through the horrors of persecution by reminding them that God was the ultimate victor in human history. Jesus himself urged us to "endure to the end" (Mt 24:13; Mk 13:13) and reminded us that the ultimate measure of success is faithfulness (Mt 25:21, 23).

Joseph exemplifies faithfulness and endurance, but it takes some digging into the text to discover this message.

Question 1. The summary in Stephen's sermon underscores the providence of God over the long haul in the life of Joseph. Over time, God used the brothers' jealousy, the famine, and the faithfulness of Joseph to redeem the people of Israel and to preserve them as the people of God.

Question 2. Have a group member read this passage in Acts 7 aloud while someone else times it. Reading these verses aloud—even slowly—usually takes less than two minutes. But the verse summary covers a period of over 100 years!

Question 3. We know from Genesis 37:2 that Joseph was seventeen when he had his dreams. Genesis 41:46 states that Joseph was thirty when he entered Pharaoh's service. We can extrapolate that Joseph spent between ages seventeen and twenty-eight first in Potiphar's house, then in prison. He was twenty-eight when the cupbearer and baker had their dreams, and two years later, he interpreted the dreams of Pharaoh. Genesis 41:53-54 adds the seven years of plenty, making Joseph thirty-seven when the seven years of famine began. In Genesis 45:6, Joseph revealed himself to his brothers—two years into the famine. He was thirty-nine years old. It had been twenty-two years since the first dream.

Question 4. The main point to make here is that Joseph endured even though he had forgotten his dream. According to his reaction to the brothers coming and his remembering his dream (Gen 42:9), we can assume that the dreams of his youth had been forgotten. Thus, his perseverance was simply plodding—following God faithfully in service to the people whom God put before him, namely the Egyptians.

Questions 5-6. The secret of Joseph's perseverance was his relationship with God, living with a daily consciousness of his presence. These questions are mostly review, but the intent is to remind group members of Joseph's relationship and dependence on God—whether in Potiphar's house, resisting temptation, serving in the prison or interpreting dreams.

Question 7. The secret of Joseph's forgiveness was his faith in the sovereignty of God. He believed that God was at work, even if he did not know how.

Questions 8-9. Try to get the group talking about what it means practically to believe that God is in control. To believe that God can bring us through the pits and prisons and betrayals of life. To forgive others because we believe that the pain they cause can be used redemptively by God. To live by faith and not by sight.

Question 10. Because Joseph endured:

- He got to see his family again, especially his brother Benjamin and his father—which in his mind was probably greater than all of Egypt's wealth and power.

- He got to see his part in the lineage of Abraham. He got to experience the blessing of his sons by Jacob (Gen 48:12-19), a very significant tradition to people of that time and place.

- He became an example of family loyalty as well as moral purity to subsequent generations and cultures. A missionary told of how African nationals were impressed with this man who "was totally loyal to his family" (Jacob Loewen, "The Gospel: Its Content and Communication," in *Down to Earth: Studies in Christianity and Culture,* ed. John Stott and Robert Coote [Grand Rapids: Eerdmans, 1980], p. 121).

- Joseph's endurance of more than twenty-two years allowed him to see the transformation in his brother Judah. Contrast Judah's speech in Genesis 44:18-34 with his angry denunciation of Joseph in Genesis 37:17-28.

- And most significantly, his faithful service in Egypt served to preserve the Messianic line.

Paul Borthwick is senior consultant for Development Associates International and previously taught at Gordon College in Wenham, Massachusetts. He dedicates himself to mobilizing others to world missions through a speaking, writing and resource ministry. He is the author of the books A Mind for Missions *(NavPress),* Six Dangerous Questions *(IVP) and one other LifeBuilder Study:* Missions.